P9-CFA-284

Traverse City
and the Beautiful Surrounding Area

Rebecca Austin & Jennifer Nelson

Austin & Nelson Publishing

104 S. Union Street, Suite 211
Traverse City, MI 49684
(616) 933-4649
aandn@aol.com

Copyright © 1997   Rebecca Austin & Jennifer Nelson

All rights reserved. No illustrations, photographs or any other portions of this book may be reproduced in any form or by any electronic or mechanical means including information storage and retrieval systems without permission in writing from the publisher except by a reviewer who may quote brief passages in a review. Austin & Nelson Publishing take no responsibility for any liability arising out of any injury of any kind which may be sustained from participation in or connection to any activities mentioned including the making or utilization of the recipes included in this publication. Every effort has been made to trace the ownership of all copyrighted picture material and subject matter. In the event of any question arising as to the use of any material or subject, the authors and publisher will be willing to make necessary corrections in future printings.

ISBN 0-9657153-0-2

First Edition

Cataloging-in-Publication

Austin, Rebecca M.
  Traverse City and the beautiful Surrounding Area / by Rebecca Austin & Jennifer Nelson. --1st ed.
    p. cm.
  ISBN 0-9657153-0-2
  1. Traverse City (Mich.)--Description and travel. 2. Leelanau County (Mich.)--Description and travel. I. Nelson, Jennifer C. II.Title.

F572.L45A87 1997   917.7'4635
                                     QBI97-40473

PRINTED IN CANADA

10 9 8 7 6 5 4 3 2 1

ACKNOWLEDGMENTS

Special thanks to The Michigan Travel Bureau, Interlochen Center for the Arts, The National Cherry Festival, Downtown Traverse City Association, Alex Moore, The Old Town Playhouse, and the Cherry Marketing Institute for their contributions.

PHOTO CREDITS

Don Rutt: Pages 6,13,16,44,48,49,50,53,54,55,56 (bottom), 59, 62, 75, 76,77 (bottom).

Dietrich Floeter: Pages 8,10,17,31,36,42,46, 56 (top), 65 (upper right & lower left), 70, back cover.

Debra Kneal: Pages 26,28,33,45,51,57,58, 61,63, 65 (upper left & lower right), 71,73.

Sally Sanders: Pages 32,52,60,68,69,72,77 (top),80.

National Cherry Festival: Pages 20,22,23,25,43.

Rebecca Austin: Pages 35,40,41,66,67.

Michigan Travel Bureau: Pages front cover, 1,14,15.

Terry W. Phipps (courtesy of Michigan Travel Bureau): Page 24.

Interlochen Center for the Arts: Pages 38,39.

Matt McCormick, Old Town Playhouse: Page 37.

Glen Rauth: Page 34.

Photeos: Page 21.

Lawrence Loesel: Page 47.

Cheryl Loesel: Back cover flap.

Maps by Nielsen Design Group.

Lovingly dedicated to my
wonderful children, Will & Layne

- Rebecca Austin

To Marilyn Nelson & Douglas Case
for their support and encouragement

- Jennifer Nelson

CONTENTS

*I*magine a place so unique it whispers romance, sings adventure and sighs relaxation all at the same time. Traverse City is a land of contrasts that appeals to many. Big city folks with demands of posh amenities are just as at home as those who are searching for the small town north woods ambiance.

The Traverse City area is an eclectic mix of natural beauty and wildlife with all the offerings of urban culture. On your way to a four star restaurant, you can stop at a farm market at the side of the road and enjoy fresh cherries. You can spend a day climbing the dunes and enjoy a cocktail at the top of a tall building at night. How about shopping at unique specialty shops in downtown Traverse City and then meeting your friends a block away for fishing at the Union Street Dam? You can in-line skate along the lake

and listen to the symphony at night. This is an area alive with exciting activities for anyone and any interest.

Situated on Northwest Michigan's beautiful lower peninsula, Traverse City's popularity as a tourist destination began in the 1800's. It is now one of the midwest's favorite destinations. Surrounded by water, the two bays make an indelible impression on visitors. Known as the "Cherry Capital of the World," Traverse City puts on a cherry celebration in July that rivals any other small town family festival in the country.

Once you visit Traverse City and the surrounding area, you'll want to come back again and again. If you're like many, you'll be dreaming of settling in Traverse City permanently.

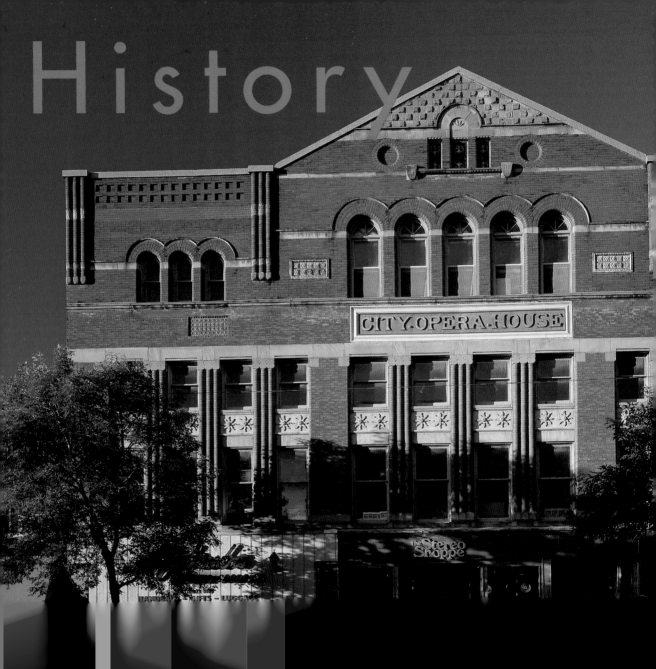

$\mathcal{T}$raverse City has a grand heritage dominated by the effects of water and trees. In the 1600's, French fur trappers crossed the large stretch of open water between Northport and Charlevoix and called it "le grande traverse" or "the great crossing."

Missionaries arrived in 1839 to work with the Ottawa and Chippewa Indians on the Old Mission Peninsula. By 1847, the first saw mill was built by Horace Boardman and within 30 years there were 16 operating lumber mills.

Evidence of these prosperous times can still be seen in the neighborhoods and buildings of downtown Traverse City. The City Opera House at 112 East Front Street, is a beautiful example. This three story red brick building opened in 1892 and is listed on the National and State Registers of Historic Places. It is one of only 18 opera houses left in Michigan. Many elegant homes from this era can still be seen in the Central and Boardman neighborhoods.

Perry Hannah, of Hannah, Lay and Company became known as the "father of Traverse City." His Hannah, Lay and Company Mercantile building can be seen at the corner of Front and Union Streets. Perry Hannah was responsible for much of the area's development including the Northern Michigan Asylum, later known as the Traverse City State Hospital. The hospital employed over 1,000 people at its peak with almost 50,000 patients. It closed in 1989, but the spires from historic Building 50 can still be seen on the west side of town.

By the 1890's, the land was stripped of both white pine and hardwood trees and the great lumber years were over. The planting of cherry and apple trees began in their place. Soon, fruit and tourism flourished in what was once a lumber baron's paradise. The first celebration of the cherries, the "Blessing of the Blossoms," was held in 1926 which developed into what is now known as the National Cherry Festival.

City dwellers from Detroit, Chicago and other midwest cities began escaping the summertime heat by staying at the lakeside resorts in and around Traverse City.

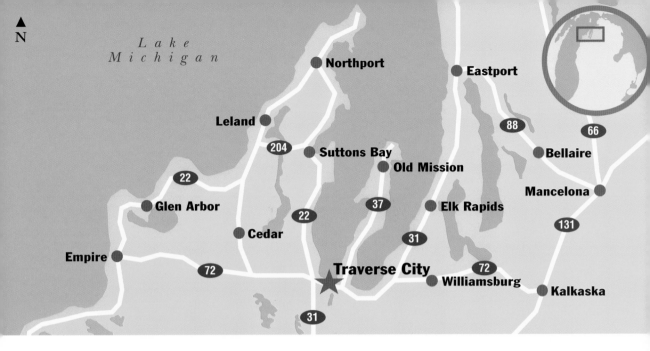

By the 1930's, tourism was growing as an industry with many stately summer cottages built as well as a new city airport. Today, tourism is the major employer.

Traditionally, winter was a quiet time with the resorts in Traverse City closing down until late spring. Downhill skiing began growing in popularity in the 1950's and 1960's. With the development of six local ski areas, Traverse City became a four season resort community.

The Traverse City area is rich in history evident in well kept architecturally interesting homes and buildings. Stroll through the neighborhoods, enjoy a carriage ride, visit the beautifully restored downtown or simply gaze at the tall ship *Malabar* on West Bay and you experience the rich heritage. Water, land and trees have shaped the growth of this beautiful area.

$\mathcal{T}$raverse City is not only Michigan's fastest growing resort community, but is also a wonderful place to live, work and raise a family. With beautiful beaches and blue skies, over 70,000 people in a five county area have chosen to have "a view of the bay with half the pay."

Traverse City is a town surrounded by water with two bays, two peninsulas and the Boardman River criss crossing through the downtown. Over one million people visit the area each year, with half a million during National Cherry Festival, which lasts for eight days in July.

Visitors and residents alike enjoy more than 30 golf courses, 50 art galleries and museums, several major shopping malls, a thriving downtown area and eight vineyards. Northern Michigan is also known for its four star gourmet restaurants and posh resorts. Traverse Citians enjoy the finest medical care available at Munson Medical Center as well as outstanding parochial, private and public schools. No longer a little northwoods town, Traverse City is a hub of commerce and tourism.

It's easy to reach Traverse City. The Cherry Capital Airport is serviced by major airlines. The beautiful drive along the east coast of Lake Michigan from Chicago is 305 miles and Detroit is only 242 miles.

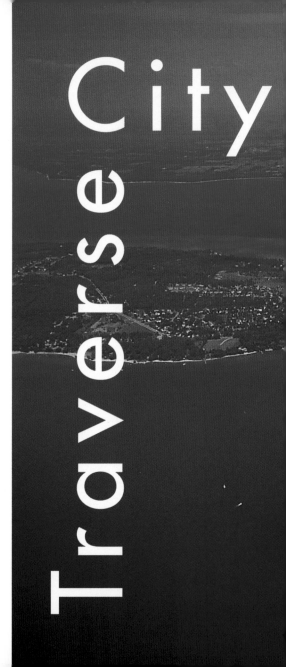

Today

One of the first cherry orchards was located near the tip of Old Mission Peninsula. Today there are more than 1,000 commercial orchards in the Grand Traverse region with over three million trees. Old Mission Peninsula, with over 500,000 trees alone, offers breathtaking views of both East and West Grand Traverse bays and cherry trees.

The surrounding large bodies of water of Grand Traverse Bay and Lake Michigan insulate the land from the extremes of weather, making an ideal area for growing cherries. The Grand Traverse area is one of the few places in the United States where such favorable conditions exist.

The combination of hilly terrain, sandy soil and conducive weather conditions makes the Traverse City area perfect for cherry growing.

Michigan produces 75% of the tart cherries grown in the United States with the Grand Traverse region producing over half of these. Cherry growing goes back to the early days of the settlers and missionaries around 1839.

Michigan produces 200 to 250 million pounds of tart cherries a year. The major variety of tart cherries grown is the Montmorency, which has been cultivated in the U.S. for more than a century. Tart cherries, which are sometimes called pie cherries or sours, are seldom sold fresh. Generally, they are canned or frozen shortly after harvest.

Sweet cherries are also grown in the Grand Traverse area. Most of them are used to make maraschino cherries. About 15% of the nation's sweet cherries come from Michigan.

Both tart and sweet cherries ripen in July with the third week of July usually the peak of the harvest. With over 160 years of cherry growing, the designation of the Grand Traverse area as the "Cherry Capital of the World" is well deserved.

*C*herries are delicious and nutritious while low in calories and sodium. With no cholesterol and practically no fat, even dieters don't have to feel guilty enjoying these luscious treats. Cherries are available canned, frozen, dried and everyone's favorite way, fresh from the tree.

There are many cherry specialty products to buy in the Traverse City area including cherry butter, cherry jam, cherry jelly, cherry mustard, cherry barbecue sauce, cherry hot pepper jelly, cherry fudge, cherry Mexican salsa, cherry pies and even cherry meat!

Plevalean

Take County Road 651 from M-72 and head north into Leelanau County until you enter the tiny town of Cedar, population 125, famous for its Cedar Polka Fest. When you get into town, ask anyone for Ray, they'll point you in the direction of Pleva's Meats, "The Sausage Capital." There you'll find Ray Pleva, working as a butcher at the very same meat market his father opened in 1919.

And it is here at this little market that Ray developed Plevalean burger, the cherry meat that has put him on national television shows like *Oprah!*, *CNN*, *Good Morning America* and even *Home Improvement* with Michigander Tim Allen.

When Ray's daughter, Cindy, was crowned the National Cherry Queen in 1987, she suggested he combine the two things he knew best, cherries and meat. Ray did just that, and now there are more than 29 meat products made with cherries including: cherry pecan pork sausage, turkey cherry sausage, cherry pepperoni snack sticks, cherry pork Canadian bacon and the now famous Plevalean burger.

Plevalean is high in protein, low in fat and cholesterol. This tasty meat has the natural flavor enhancer of cherries, is juicy and has half the calories of regular hamburger. It is being sold nationally now and has won numerous awards.

As offered by the Cherry Marketing Institute, Inc.

Cherry Oatmeal Muffins

Perfect for breakfast on the run or lunch box treats

1 cup old-fashioned or quick-cooking oats, uncooked
1 cup all-purpose flour
1/2 cup firmly packed brown sugar
1 1/2 teaspoons baking powder
1/4 teaspoon ground nutmeg
3/4 cup buttermilk
1 egg, slightly beaten
1/4 cup vegetable oil
1 teaspoon almond extract
1 cup frozen tart cherries, coarsely chopped

In a large mixing bowl, combine oats, flour, brown sugar, baking powder and nutmeg.

In a small bowl, combine buttermilk, egg, oil and almond extract. Pour buttermilk mixture into oats mixture; stir just to moisten ingredients. Quickly stir in cherries (it is not necessary to thaw the cherries before chopping and adding to the batter).

Spray muffin pan with non-stick spray. Fill muffin cups 2/3 full and bake in pre-heated 400 degree oven for 15-20 minutes.

Makes 12 muffins

Nutritional information per muffin: 159 calories, 5.6 grams total fat, 18 mg cholesterol, 61 mg sodium

Maple Cherry Sauce

Just right for roast chicken, game birds or holiday turkey or goose.

1 medium orange
1 can (16 oz) tart cherries, drained or
1 1/2 cups frozen tart cherries
1 cup maple syrup
1 cup cherry juice blend or apple-cherry juice
1/2 cup coarsely chopped walnuts, optional

Rinse orange and remove any blemishes from the rind. Grate rind until you have about 1/3 cup. Save remaining orange for another use.

In a large saucepan, combine grated orange rind, cherries, maple syrup and juice. Cover and bring mixture to a rolling boil, then lower heat and simmer 10 minutes to blend flavors. Remove from heat and stir in walnuts, if desired. Cool, then cover and refrigerate. Sauce will keep 3 to 4 days; re-heat before serving.

Makes 12 servings

Nutritional information per serving with walnuts: 103 calories, .08 grams total fat, 0 mg cholesterol, 4 mg sodium

$\mathcal{A}$s one of the nation's "Top Ten Festivals" as noted in 1996 in *USA Today*, the National Cherry Festival began as the "Blessing of the Blossoms" in 1926. Farmers everywhere are at the mercy of the weather and these early cherry farmers, no doubt, wanted all the help they could get! The National Cherry Festival has for over 70 years been celebrating the passion of the cherry fruit.

Each year, the festival hosts more than 150 activities and events for the entire family including three parades, sporting events, band

onal Cherry Festival

competitions, big name entertainment, air shows, fireworks, the crowning of the queen and the ever popular midway rides, all in the heart of Traverse City.

Children love the many events scheduled all week including a cherry pie eating contest, chalk art competition, turtle races, big wheel race, pet parade, bubble gum blowing contest, bike rodeo and even a sand sculpturing contest on the beach.

Adults have as much fun at the bike race, 15K foot race, beach volleyball tournaments, bed race and the hole in one contest. All ages love the parades. The Heritage Parade on Tuesday evening highlights the history of the area and the Junior Royale Parade on Thursday evening is designed especially for children. One of the largest parades in the midwest, the Cherry Royale Parade is held on Saturday and features 150 entries.

The Festival utilizes a corps of more than 800 local volunteers with over 30,000 man hours to put together the massive event. The center of activity is the downtown "Open Space" which holds the music pavilion, food tents and a "Cherry Pavilion" with all kinds of cherry products. Nearby is the midway and arts and crafts show.

A giant fireworks display over West Grand Traverse Bay on the last evening of the festival is a beautiful finale of color. Hundreds of boats bob in the bay while the colors light up the sky to thousands of onlookers.

The National Cherry Festival has not only enjoyable events but it also has a mission to give back to the community. Proceeds from the festival help to fund over 40 non-profit organizations. The National Cherry Festival is great for visitors and supports the community at the same time.

Downtown

ree lined sidewalks with park benches along century old brick pavement form pedestrian friendly East Front Street, Downtown, Traverse City. There are over 200 specialty shops, coffee shops and gourmet restaurants, many housed in beautifully restored turn-of-the-century buildings. Traverse City's downtown is a thriving, active area popular with tourists and residents alike that reminds one of a small town of yesteryear.

Year round events take place like "Friday Night Live" when the downtown is closed to car traffic each Friday evening from the end of July through September 1st. Families enjoy performers and dancing, art activities, even rides on a vintage fire engine. At Christmas time, the lighting of a huge downtown Christmas tree and the singing of Christmas carols, ring in the beginning of the holiday season.

The Boardman River is closed to boat traffic for the annual "Classic Boats on the Boardwalk," a display of more than 100 antique and classic wood boats along the river boardwalk in August. The "Tall Ship Rally" each summer commences from the Open Space offering a rare view of three grand tall ship schooner replicas sailing all together on West Grand Traverse Bay.

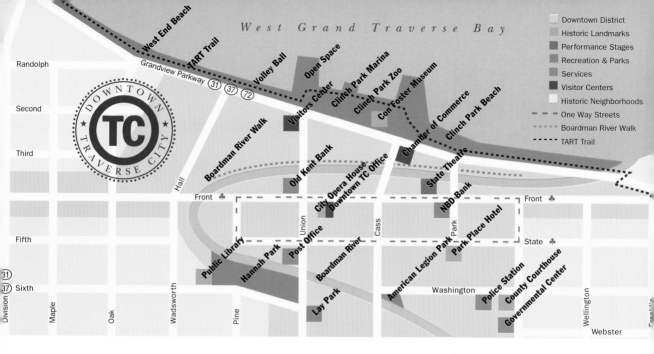

The small town character has been preserved with a respect for history. Take a walk past the historic courthouse on the corner of Washington and Boardman Streets. The ten story Park Place Hotel at Park and State Streets, was originally established in 1873 as The Campbell House. The Park Place Hotel is one of the most recognizable landmarks downtown. While strolling downtown, look up at the building facades and notice many with engraved dates and old Traverse City founding family names. Olde Town Traverse City, on Union Street, also has shops in historic buildings.

Within walking distance from Front Street are the Clinch Park Beach and Marina and the Clinch Park Zoo. The zoo is set on 3.5 acres and features a train ride that is a favorite with the kids. The Con Foster Museum offers historical displays and changing exhibits. The Open Space on West Grand Traverse Bay serves as the base for the National Cherry Festival each July, and also as a great place to relax or fly a kite. The T.A.R.T., Traverse Area Recreational Trail, crosses through downtown, and the Riverwalk along the Boardman River is beautiful.

Traverse City Events

February
Red Hot Chili Cookoff-The Opera House
North American VASA-Acme

April
Noon Notes- The Opera House

May
Downtown Farmers Market Opens Through September
Northwestern Michigan College Barbecue

June
Tall Ship Rally on West Grand Traverse Bay
Ribs, Bibs, Tall Ships and Kids- Clinch Park/Open Space
Olde Town Merchants Bazaar- Union Street in Olde Town
Old-Fashioned Family Fun Day- Clinch Park Zoo

July
The National Cherry Festival
Cherry Festival Fireworks Finale

August
Friday Night Live
Classic Boats on the Boardwalk
Downtown Street Sale
Downtown Traverse City Art Fair
Sidewalk Art Project- Union Street, Olde Town
(Saturdays)
Artists Market- Farmers Market at Cass & Grandview
(Sundays)

September
Cherry Classic Car Show

October
Happy Apple Days

November
Santa's Arrival and Christmas Tree Lighting
Festival of Trees- Dennos Museum Center

December
Christmas for the Animals- Clinch Park Zoo
Festival of Trains- The Opera House

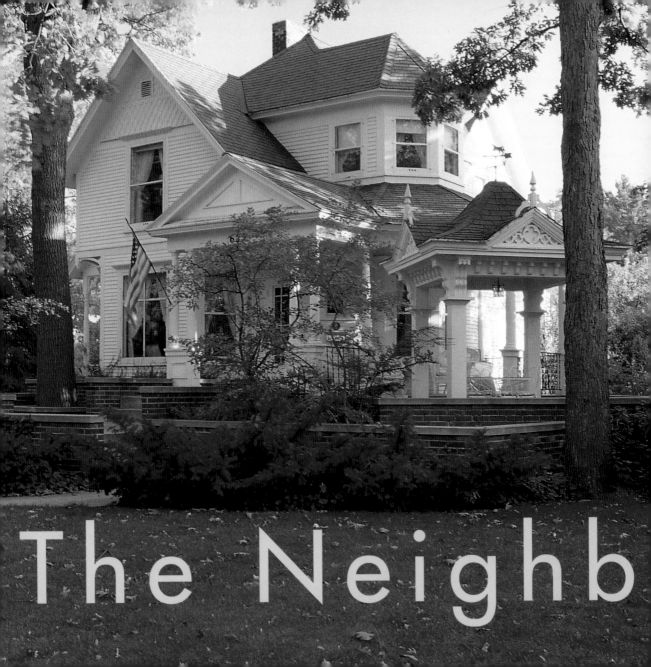

The Neighb

Traverse City developed as a typical lumber town. The town had over 20 saloons, all crowded with lumberjacks and sawmill workers. Sleder's Tavern, one of the oldest continually operating taverns in the state, is still much as it was in 1882. Located on Randolph Street, on the west side, it is surrounded by the modest homes of these original lumber workers.

The successful professionals and civic leaders developed two elegant neighborhoods, Boardman and Central. Both are showcases of Victorian homes with ornate woodwork and stained glass windows in many styles of architecture. Beautiful examples of Italianate, Queen Anne, Georgian Revival and Stick style homes can be seen throughout these neighborhoods. Many are still single family homes.

orhood

The Boardman Historic District includes 170 structures listed on the State Historical Register with most built between 1870 and 1910. The neighborhood is bordered by State, Railroad, and Webster Streets and Boardman Avenue. Replicas of the original gas lights line the streets making it a pleasant walking tour neighborhood. Don't miss the historic Oval Wood Dish Company founder home at the corner of Washington and Wellington Streets.

The Central Neighborhood Historic District lies near the business district along the Boardman River and is bounded by Fifth, Locust, Union, Ninth and Division Streets. It was the second fashionable neighborhood. Most homes were built between 1890 and 1914 and include the Perry Hannah House at 305 Sixth Street, a premier example of Victorian architecture. Perry Hannah of Hannah, Lay and Company platted much of the neighborhood and donated land for the library, school and park. More than 50 structures in the neighborhood have been identified with historical merit.

Traverse City has earned a reputation as the cultural mecca of Northern Michigan. The 40,000 square foot Dennos Museum Center and Milliken Auditorium at Northwestern Michigan College offers changing exhibits four times a year including contemporary works and a permanent collection of Inuit Eskimo Art. The Milliken Auditorium offers music, dance, theatre and lecture events. Children can experience hands on activities in science, art and technology at the Museum's Discovery Center. The Dennos Museum also offers educational programs, tours and a museum store.

Two theatre groups, the Michigan Ensemble Theatre, a professional summer theatre group, and the Traverse City Civic Players at the Old Town Playhouse, offer outstanding dramatic entertainment.

The Traverse Symphony Orchestra produces major performances of symphonic music. Traverse City boasts a thriving jazz scene with performances live in clubs that rival any city.

Two groups, the Traverse Area Arts Council, located in the Opera House and the Northwestern Michigan Artists and Craftsmen, support an active community of visual artists.

The Traverse Bay Area Art Fair is held the last Saturday of July at Northwestern Michigan College and offers a chance to see the high quality work from many artists.

The Olde Town Bazaar held in June on Union Street features 100 artists and craftsmen. Each Sunday in August the Artist Market is held downtown.

For those that like to get in the car and go on a tour of antique shops, the area offers more than 30 shops as well as four major antique malls. Art galleries and artists' studios abound featuring pottery, jewelry, sculpture, watercolors and photography.

History lovers will enjoy the museums that focus on regional lore such as the Con Foster Museum at Clinch Park. For music history buffs, The Music House in Acme features restored rare antique musical instruments including organs, radios, phonographs, music boxes and nickelodeons.

ARTS

Interlochen

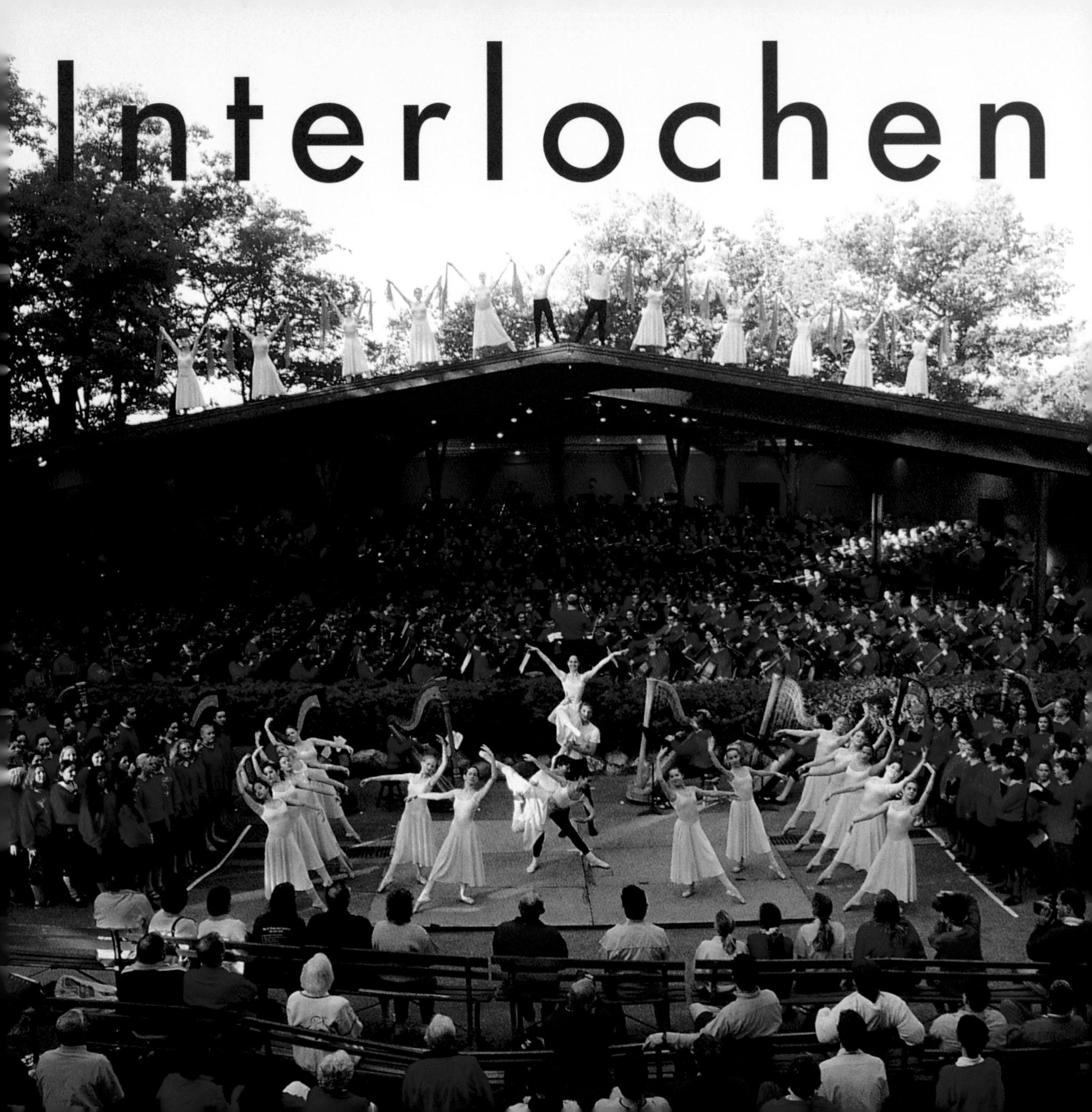

The little town of Interlochen, located 14 miles southwest of Traverse City, has a big reputation. Located between Green and Duck Lakes, it is home to Interlochen Center for the Arts, the nation's oldest, largest and best known center for the performing arts.

World class arts education is offered through Interlochen Arts Academy, a full academic program, and is considered the premier fine arts high school in the country. Interlochen Arts Camp features four and eight week summer programs for students eight to eighteen to study music, theatre arts, dance, creative writing and visual arts.

The Interlochen Center for the Arts umbrella organization has also grown to include Interlochen Public Radio, one of the top public radio stations in the country. The Interlochen Arts Festival presents more than 750 concerts and exhibits annually from students, faculty and some of the nation's preeminent artists.

Situated on a 1,200 acre campus surrounded by clear blue lakes and pine trees, Interlochen Center for the Arts is the cultural jewel of the north.

The scenic Old Mission Peninsula stretches north through 14 miles of rolling hills, cherry orchards, vineyards and groves of stately old maple trees. Offering outstanding views of both East and West Grand Traverse Bays, the drive is a wonderful way to see thousands of cherry trees with blossoms in the spring and is one of the best choices for a color tour in the fall.

Along the drive on M-37, you'll find charming restaurants, farm fruit stands in season and wineries. At the tip of the peninsula, visit the historic lighthouse. The Old Mission Lighthouse, built in 1870, has a beautiful sand beach that stretches for miles and is great for hiking and picnicking. Right in the town of Old Mission, stands a replica of the original mission established in 1842 to serve the Chippewa and Ottawa Indian tribes.

The town of Old Mission lies on the 45th parallel, half way between the equator and the North Pole. Four outstanding wineries on the peninsula offer tasting rooms and incredible views. What a coincidence that the Bordeaux region of France, another famous wine region, also rests on the 45th parallel! Don't miss Old Mission's celebration of "Blossom Days" in May.

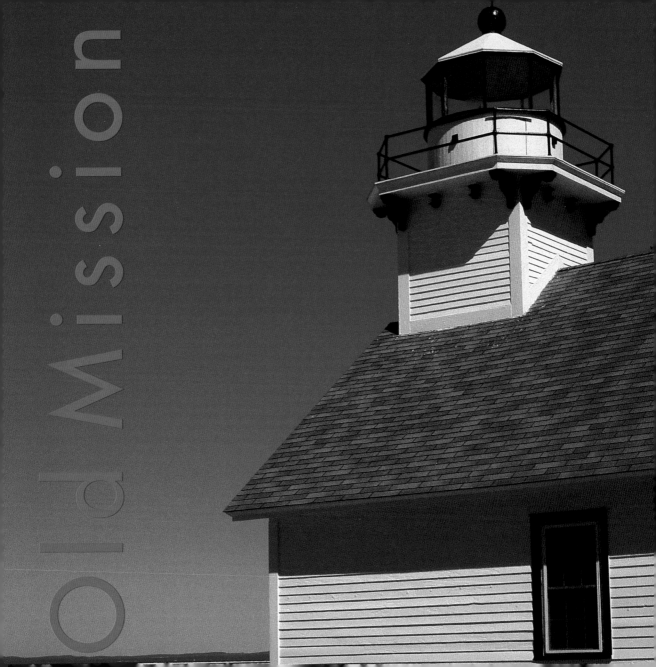

old Mission

Summertime

If you love the water, the Traverse City Area is the place to be with miles of Lake Michigan shoreline, numerous inland lakes and at least five exceptional rivers. Crystal clean water, fresh air and blue skies makes the nations' "third coast" a water lover's paradise.

Two beaches are within a short walk of the downtown shopping area in Traverse City. The West End beach is known for its beach volley-ball tournaments. The Clinch Park beach is most widely known for bikinis and musclemen and is close to the Clinch Park Zoo. Bryant Park, at the base of the Old Mission Peninsula, is a prime sunset spot as well as a great beach

choice for families with small children. On East Grand Traverse Bay, East Bay Park beach, near Northwestern Michigan College, is warm and shallow. Tony Gilroy Township Park beach on the east shore is a haven for windsurfers.

For those who want quite and solitude, Lake Michigan beaches offer many choices. At Sleeping Bear Dunes National Lakeshore, Good Harbor, North Bar Lake or Old Mission Peninsula's Lighthouse Park, you can enjoy pure white sand, blue skies and a romantic place to watch the sunset.

These beaches are also good places to hunt for Petoskey stones, the state stone. These elusive petrified corral fossils have a gray, hexagonal pattern that comes alive when wet.

There's a water adventure suited for everyone in the Grand Traverse area. Rent a power or sail boat, ride the waves on a jet ski, canoe, kayak, tube or raft down the rivers or skin dive for an underwater adventure. If you love antique and classic wood boats, don't miss the "Classic Boats on the Boardwalk" in August on the Riverwalk downtown.

For a mix of maritime history, sailing and sightseeing, there are three picturesque tall ships that sail on Lake Michigan and West Grand Traverse Bay. The *Malabar* is an authentic replica of a 19th century schooner and offers cruises. The *Manitou*, out of Northport Harbor, and The *Madeline*, built and used by the Maritime Heritage Alliance for education on the Great Lakes, are also schooners that offer tours. All three tall ships meet together in June for a sailing event called "Ribs, Bibs, Tall Ships and Kids" on West Grand Traverse Bay.

If you aren't a water lover, the area still offers many other activities. The Traverse Area Recreational Trail (T.A.R.T.) is an eight-foot wide asphalt path which shares a railroad right-of-way. The non-motorized trail begins along West End Beach near M-72 and continues to East Grand Traverse Bay and the village of Acme. Bikers, in-line skaters, runners and walkers enjoy the ten miles of scenic trail which passes both bays and meanders through woods and past streams.

The hills surrounding Traverse City offer premier mountain biking terrain coupled with scenic views. For those that prefer touring bike trips, the Pierce Stocking Drive in the Sleeping Bear Dunes National Lakeshore Park offers seven miles of hills to peddle.

Summertime is fruit time in the Grand Traverse area with not only the famous cherries but also apples, peaches, blueberries and strawberries to enjoy. On your way to the beach or for a bike tour, you are sure to pass an orchard store, fruit stand or farm market. Even in downtown Traverse City on the corner of Front and Park Streets, you can enjoy the seasonal parade of fruit at Selkirk's. The Farmer's Market on the Boardman River between Union and Cass Streets, is open every Wednesday and Saturday in the summer with every fresh vegetable and fruit in season. Leelanau County is full of markets and you can still find many of the honor system fruit stands in front of centennial farms.

The Traverse City area is considered the golf mecca of the midwest with more than 40 courses to choose. With the panoramic views of spectacular hill and lake country, some say it's tough to keep your eye on the ball. Thanks to the balmy and breezy weather in the north, conditions are ideal when the rest of the midwest is sweltering. The late northern summer sun makes twilight golf a joy well past 9:00 p.m. Golfers can tee off at 5:00 p.m. and still play 18 holes!

Whether you enjoy a casual stroll, star gazing and relaxing or high adventure and rugged outdoor action, you'll find it in the Traverse City area in summertime.

FALL

Fall means color tour time in the Traverse City area. Farm markets are full with blackberries, pears, plums, apples and grapes. Roadside vegetable stands offer festive displays of pumpkins, gourds, squash and ears of colored corn. Warm up with donuts and hot cider on a break from touring at a cider mill.

Color changes peak anytime from late September to mid-October. Take a drive along M-22 on the Leelanau Peninsula along the shoreline of West Grand Traverse Bay through the quaint port villages of Suttons Bay, Omena and Northport. Lighthouses with hiking trails through the woods can be found at Old Mission Peninsula and north of Northport at the Grand Traverse Lighthouse. The Pierce Stocking Drive within the National Lakeshore Park, offers beautiful colors coupled with scenic turnoffs and overlooks of Lake Michigan.

Canoeing provides a color tour with a different perspective. Meandering leisurely down any of the local rivers, Crystal, Boardman, Betsie or Platte, lets you enjoy the color of the red maples reflected in the water with the added possibility of catching sight of a loon or wild geese.

Fall is an ideal time for a bike tour to enjoy the marvelous colors. The Leelanau Trail follows M-22 from Greilickville to Suttons Bay along the old railroad bed for 15 scenic miles.

Everyone associates Northern Michigan with cherries, but it is also wine country. The moderating effect of Lake Michigan which helps to make the area a prime cherry growing spot also works in grape production. The cool weather in spring holds back the vine production while the lakes store up the summer heat, extending the growing season in the autumn. The lake-effect snows in winter provide an insulating barrier to the tender grapevine roots.

There are four wineries on Old Mission Peninsula; Bowers Harbor Vineyards, Chateau Chantal, Chateau Grand Traverse and Old Mission Cellars. Leelanau County also has four with Boskydel Vineyards, Good Harbor Vineyards, Leelanau Wine Cellars and L. Mawby Winery. Most offer tasting rooms and educational information not to mention spectacular views.

A color tour would not be complete without a stop at a cider mill. You can view actual cider being pressed at the Hitchpoint Cider Mill in Williamsburg. The only horse powered cider press in Michigan, Hitchpoint uses Norwegian Fjord horses to turn the huge press. Kids can enjoy a pony ride, fresh cider and homemade donuts. Amon Orchards just north of the intersection of M-72 and US-31, offers trolley rides through the orchards, a barnyard petting zoo and delicious cinnamon rolls fresh from their bakery.

Favorite Color Tours

The Leelanau Peninsula
About 93 Miles

Take M-22 north to Northport. Then continuing south along the western side of the Peninsula through Leland and Glen Arbor. Take M-109 to the dune climb and Pierce Stocking Drive. Take M-22 to Empire and then left on M-72 back to Traverse City.

The Old Mission Peninsula
About 38 miles

At Garfield Road go north on Peninsula Drive. When the road forks keep right on M-37 and continue 14 miles to the very tip of the Peninsula and find the lighthouse. To return, go west on Bowers Harbor Road and follow Peninsula Drive along the West Bay back to Traverse City.

Benzie County
About 64 Miles

Take US-31/M-37 south from Traverse City to the intersection of M-37 and US-31 about eight miles, also called Chum's Corners. Turn right on US-31, then left on M-137. Continue on M-137 to C-700 and turn right in the village of Karlin. Make a right on County Line Road to Thompsonville and then right on M-115 to Benzonia and Beulah. Loop back on to US-31 North and make a left turn at Chum's Corners back to Traverse City.

Wintertime

*B*lessed by 150 to 200 inches of snow every winter, the area offers a wealth of winter recreation. With ample snowfall combined with huge blocks of public land, miles of well maintained trails and resorts offering many activities, there is no reason to hide from the weather in Northern Michigan. Snow begins around Thanksgiving and continues with good conditions well into March.

Traverse City is a downhill skier's and snow boarder's paradise with two ski areas right in Traverse City. The city of Traverse City owns Hickory Hills, a ski hill on the west side of town. Mount Holiday, a private ski hill on the east side make getting on the slopes just a

matter of minutes from downtown. Three resorts within an hour drive include Crystal Mountain in Thompsonville, Sugar Loaf in Cedar and The Homestead in Glen Arbor, all offering novice to expert runs. The combination of natural and man-made snow ensures superb conditions. There are few places in the U.S. where skiers and boarders can look out at beautiful clear blue water while shussing the slopes.

Some of the best cross-country skiing around the Great Lakes can be had in Northern Michigan with both public and resort trails for traditional and free style skiing. Two of the largest cross-country races in North America are held on back to back weekends in February; the White Pine Stampede with 20K and 50K events and the North American VASA with 10K, 25K and 45K events.

For those who like the quiet serenity of traditional cross-country trails and rustic solitude, the Muncie Lakes Pathway, Leelanau State Park, Old Mission Lighthouse, Sand Lakes Quiet Area and the Sleeping Bear National Lakeshore areas are perfect. Bring along a thermos of hot chocolate and a picnic lunch in a backpack and escape the crowds.

For snowmobilers, the Boardman Valley system offers five staging areas and over 81 miles of trails winding through the Pere Marquette Forest. Ample snowfall, well maintained and marked trails and secluded forests full of fox and deer make it a snowmobilers' delight.

A host of events and festivals fill the days of winter. Thousands of twinkling lights decorate the grounds at the Grand Traverse Resort and inside, children will delight in the animated winter scenes. The "Festival of Trees" held at the Dennos Museum presents a magnificent display of over 100 decorated trees and wreaths. Santa arrives downtown for the lighting of a huge Christmas tree and leads carolers in singing.

The winter wonderland wouldn't be complete without sleigh rides at the resorts, ice skating in Traverse City on Fourteenth Street, snowshoeing, sledding and ice fishing. Residents of Traverse City embrace the winter and its snow, reveling in the many activities.

Spring is a time of anxiously awaited returns, return of the wildflowers, the robins and sunny days. Winter in Northern Michigan is often a five-month-long season and even the most avid snow lover looks forward to the awakening of spring.

Morels, the sponge headed mushrooms sometimes called the "truffles of the north," bring the nature lovers to the woods in droves around late April and early May. These delicacies are inconspicuous to the point of being invisible to the average woods stalker, which makes them all the more delightful when found. Morels are the reason for many festivals and celebrations. Top morellers sell their mushrooms for as much as $15.00 per pound to local restaurants.

While in the woods, look for the beautiful trillium flowers, a protected species of wildflower. The trillium lies low to the floor of the woods with small, delicate white petals.

Spring is a quiet season and a perfect time to catch sight of loons whose mournful cry alerts you to its presence. Known as the bird who mates for life, there are now more than 500 known pairs existing in the state with many in Northern Michigan.

Spring

Buffalo have become a popular part of the tourist scene in Traverse City. In 1954, Gerald Oleson, founder of the Oleson's Food Store chain, decided to become a buffalo rancher after the flavorful meat from the west sold well in his stores. He started with 20 buffalo and today the herd now numbers over 600. Now known as the largest buffalo herd east of the Mississippi River, you can see part of the herd on US-31 South. Don't miss the giant buffalo head mounted on the wall at the original wood floored Oleson's Store at 901 West Front Street in Traverse City.

Northern Michigan is also famous across the U.S. for its trout streams. The Boardman, Platte and Betsie Rivers offer brook and brown trout in abundance to the fly fisherman. Early April brings brown trout, steelhead and salmon into the shallow water and can be caught from a small boat or casting from shore. The glacial formed inland lakes of the region, not only being some of the most beautiful, are also home to pike, bass and walleye. Try Silver, Crystal, Long, Big Glen or North Lake Leelanau for a good fishing spot.

LEELANAU
COUNTY

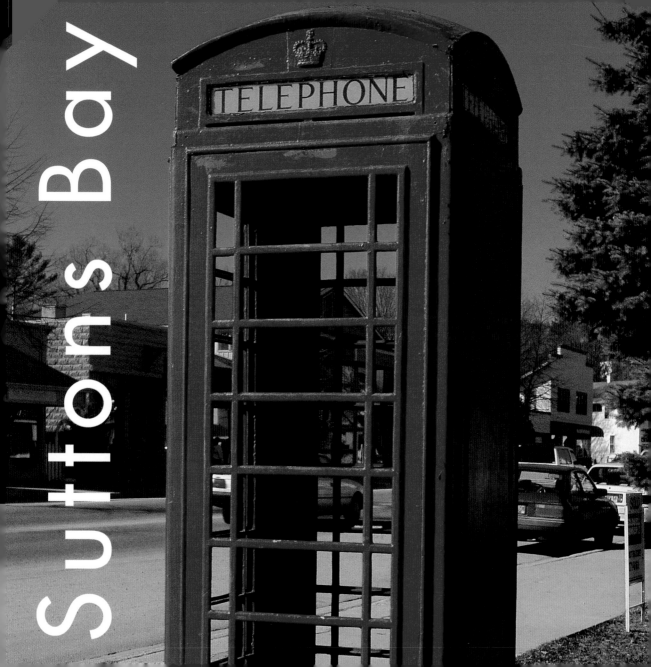

*I*n 1854, Harry C. Sutton settled with a crew of woodsmen to supply fuel for the woodburning steamboats that harbored in the bay and thus Suttons Bay was born. Today, this quaint, old Victorian era town has a thriving harbor, big old houses and an eclectic mix of boutiques and galleries.

Visit the Bay Theatre, which shows first run, art and foreign films. Bahle's Department store, run by the fourth generation of a founding Suttons Bay family, has remained at the same location since 1876. A restored fire station, built around 1913, now houses a restaurant. Bright red antique telephone booths on the corners add a whimsical touch to this tiny town.

The village has many community events including the Classic Wood Boat Show in June, the Jazz Fest in July, the Art Festival in August, and at holiday time the "Christmas in the Village" events.

The Leelanau Trail links Traverse City and Suttons Bay along an old railroad right-of-way, offering bikers and walkers a scenic, quiet path for 15 miles. Just north of Suttons Bay, the Leelanau Sands Casino attracts bus loads of gamblers all year long.

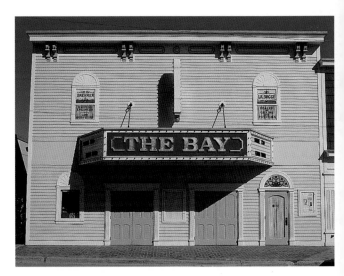

$\mathcal{N}$orthport is the most northern village on the Leelanau Peninsula and is well worth the drive. The Grand Traverse Lighthouse, located nine miles north of the village on the very tip of the point, is on the National and State Registers of Historic Sites. The lighthouse operates as a maritime museum within the 1,300 acre Leelanau State Park system. The park offers rustic camping and plenty of beach to comb for Petoskey stones.

Northport celebrates "Harbor Days" in July, "Music in the Park" on Fridays in July at Haserot Park and a wine festival in August.

LELAND

On a narrow sliver of land between Lake Leelanau and Lake Michigan lies the 140 year old fishing village of Leland. A short stretch of river connects the two lakes and flows over a dam leading to the area of town known as "Fishtown."

A double row of historic fishing shanties lies on both sides of the river, all built between 1900 and 1930. These gray, weathered shanties were constructed by the fishermen to house their equipment, repair nets and store ice. They remain today, largely unchanged. A few are still in use by commercial fishermen offering fresh and smoked fish direct from Lake Michigan. Most now house tiny gift shops and galleries.

Charter fishing trips and excursions to the North and South Manitou Islands commence from the harbor in Leland. Don't miss the Leland Wine and Food Festival in June. The area boasts a number of gourmet restaurants like The Bluebird and The Cove as well as award winning vineyards and wineries.

Glen Arbor

Situated on Sleeping Bear Bay, Glen Arbor lies on the mile wide strip of land that separates Glen Lake from Lake Michigan. Quaint shops and restaurants make it a pleasant stop after visiting the dunes. The scenic overlook on Miller Hill Road is worth the small detour for the fabulous view.

The village of Empire, once a lumber town, is still picturesque with its Victorian store fronts. North Bar Lake, three miles north of the village, a secluded lake with a small stream that connects it to Lake Michigan, is a favorite for its romantic sunsets. Empire holds its "Dunegrass and Blues Festival" in August each year.

EMPIRE

The 70,000 acre Sleeping Bear Dunes National Lakeshore park is located about 30 miles from Traverse City. The park encompasses 21 inland lakes; two navigable rivers, the Platte and Crystal; two islands, North and South Manitou; and 30 miles of shore frontage. All this beauty is within 100 square miles.

The last Ice Age glacier retreated more than 11,000 years ago leaving behind Lake Michigan, many smaller lakes and a sandy coast of ever shifting dunes. Growth of beach grass, wild grapes and wildflowers help to stabilize the moving sand. The Sleeping Bear Dunes is believed to be the largest live fresh water dunes in the world.

Chippewa Indian legend describes the formation of the dunes differently. Legend has it that a mother bear and her two cubs tried to swim across the great expanse of Lake Michigan from Wisconsin in order to escape a great fire. The mother made it across and lay down on the shore to sleep and await her cubs. The little cubs were too exhausted and soon drowned off shore.

Sleeping

Bear Dunes

NATIONAL LAKESHORE

The great Indian spirit, *Manitou*, raised the cubs from the water and they are the two islands you now see, North and South Manitou.

South Manitou Island is known for its "Valley of the Giants," a grove of more than 400-year-old white cedar trees. The freighter *Francisco Morazon* was wrecked and sunk off the shore of South Manitou in 1960 and can be seen from the south shore. There are many other shipwrecks around the islands that provide great dive sites for divers.

The dunes rise 460 feet above the level of Lake Michigan. The Pierce Stocking Scenic Drive traverses more than seven miles across the dunes with scenic overlooks and markers for historical and natural features of interest. The drive twists through a beech and maple forest and is lovely in all four seasons. The Sleeping Bear Dunes are considered one of the great natural treasures of our area.

NUMBERS TO KNOW

Visitor Information

Traverse City Convention and Visitors Bureau
Information on fall color tour, antique shops, motor and hiking tours, hotels, restaurants and events
101 West Grandview Parkway
Traverse City, 49684
800-TRAVERS (800-872-8377)

Downtown Traverse City Association
112 1/2 East Front Street
Traverse City, 49684
(616) 922-2050

National Cherry Festival
108 West Grandview Parkway
Traverse City, 49684
(616) 947-4230

Leland Business Association
Main Street
Leland, 49654
(616) 256-9900

Travel Michigan
P.O. Box 30226
Lansing, 48909
(800) 543-2937

Recreation

T.A.R.T.
(Traverse Area Recreational Trail)
(616) 933-8278 or 941-BIKE

North American VASA
4450 Bartlett, Acme 49690
(616) 938-4400

White Pine Stampede
103 East State Street
Mancelona, 49659
(616) 587-8812

Chambers of Commerce

Traverse City
202 East Grandview Parkway
Traverse City, 49684
(616) 947-5075

Interlochen
2502 South M-137
Interlochen, 49643
(616) 276-7141

Leelanau County
105 East Philip
Lake Leelanau, 49653
(616) 256-9895

Suttons Bay
105 East Philip
Lake Leelanau, 49653
(616) 271-5077

Northport and Omena
109 West Nagonabe
Northport, 49670
(616) 386-5806

Glen Lake
5669 Manitou
Glen Arbor, 49636
(616) 334-3238

Empire
105 East Philip
Lake Leelanau, 49653
(616) 326-5287

Education

Interlochen Center For the Arts
M - 137, P.O.Box 199
Interlochen, 49643
(616) 276-7200

Northwestern Michigan College
1701 East Front Street
Traverse City, 49686
(616) 922-1000

Arts & Museums

Dennos Museum Center
Northwestern Michigan College
1701 East Front Street
Traverse City, 49686
(616) 922-1055

Con Foster Museum
US 31 and Cass Street
Traverse City, 49684
(616) 922-4905

Leelanau County Historical Museum
203 East Cedar Street
Leland, 49654
(616) 256-7475

Empire Area Museum
LaCore Street, M-22
Empire, 49630
(616) 326-5568 or (616) 326-5181

Sleeping Bear Maritime Museum
M - 109 near Glen Haven
(616) 326-5134

Michigan Ensemble Theatre
Wellington and State Streets
Traverse City, 49686
(616) 929-7260

Old Town Playhouse and Traverse City Civic Players
148 East Eighth Street
Traverse City, 49686
(616) 947-2210

Traverse Symphony Orchestra
123 1/2 East Front Street
Traverse City, 49684
(616) 947-7120

Arts & Museums Continued

Traverse Area Arts Council and Gallery
106 1/2 East Front Street
Traverse City, 49684
(616) 947-2282

Northwestern Michigan Artists and Craftsmen
720 South Elmwood
Traverse City, 49684
(616) 941-9488

City Opera House
112 1/2 East Front Street
Traverse City, 49684
(616) 922-2070

Parks and Lighthouses

Clinch Park Zoo
161 Grandview Parkway
West Grand Traverse Bay
Traverse City, 49684
(616) 922-4904

Sleeping Bear Dunes National Lakeshore
9922 Front Street (Highway 72)
Empire, 49630
(616) 326-5134

Old Mission Lighthouse
Tip of the Old Mission Peninsula
Old Mission, 49673

Grand Traverse Lighthouse
Leelanau State Park
15390 County Road 629
Northport, 49670
(616) 386-9145 or (616) 386-5825

Michigan State Park Campgrounds
Traverse City, Interlochen, Leelanau
(800) 44-PARKS

INDEX